ROMAN CITY
GUIDEBOOK

Jill Laidlaw

Crabtree Publishing Company

www.crabtreebooks.com

Author: Jill Laidlaw
Editor: Crystal Sikkens
Project coordinator: Kathy Middleton
Production coordinator: Ken Wright
Prepress technician: Margaret Amy Salter
Series consultant: Gill Matthews

Picture credits:
Alamy: The London Art Archive 20
Bridgeman Art Library: Heini Schneebeli 18,
    Verulamium Museum 21
Corbis: Vanni Archive 4
Fotolia: (Cover) Tinka
Istockphoto: (Cover) Thomas Pullicino 15b
Photoshot: De Agostini/World Illustrated 13
Rex Features: Collection 12, Sipa Press 11
Shutterstock: (Cover) Cornel Achirei, Ljupco Smokovski,
    Pippa West; Danilo Ascione 7t, Matthew Collingwood 19,
    Dragunov 17t, Laurence Gough 8l, Gul 5, Javarman 10b,
    Marivlada 10t, Massimo Merlini 16, Andre Nantel 14,
    Clara Natoli 15t, 17b, Kenneth V. Pilon 9t,
    Ruta Saulyte-Laurinaviciene 9b, Tomasz Szymanski 8r,
    Khirman Vladimir 7b
Illustration: Geoff Ward 6

Every effort has been made to trace copyright holders and to obtain their permission for use of copyright material. The authors and publishers would be pleased to rectify any error or omission in future editions. All the Internet addresses given in this book were correct at the time of going to press. The author and publishers regret any inconvenience caused if addresses have changed or sites have ceased to exist, but can accept no responsibility for any such changes.

Library and Archives Canada Cataloguing in Publication

Laidlaw, Jill A.
    Roman city guidebook / Jill Laidlaw.

(Crabtree connections)
Includes index.
ISBN 978-0-7787-9949-8 (bound).--ISBN 978-0-7787-9971-9 (pbk.)

    1. Rome (Italy)--History--To 476--Juvenile literature.
2. Rome (Italy)--Social life and customs--Juvenile literature.
3. Rome--Social life and customs--Juvenile literature.
I. Title. II. Series: Crabtree connections.

DG33.L33 2010   j937.63   C2010-901514-2

Library of Congress Cataloging-in-Publication Data

Laidlaw, Jill A.
    Roman city guidebook / Jill Laidlaw.
        p. cm. -- (Crabtree connections)
    Includes index.
    ISBN 978-0-7787-9949-8 (reinforced lib. bdg. : alk. paper)
    -- ISBN 978-0-7787-9971-9 (pbk. : alk. paper)
    1. Rome (Italy)--History--To 476--Juvenile literature. 2. Rome (Italy)
--Social life and customs--Juvenile literature. 3. Rome--Juvenile
literature. 4. Rome--Social life and customs--Juvenile literature. I.
Title. II. Series.

    DG77.L246 2010
    937'.63--dc22
                                                    2010008056

Crabtree Publishing Company

www.crabtreebooks.com   1-800-387-7650

Printed in the U.S.A./062010/WO20100815

Published in Canada
Crabtree Publishing
616 Welland Ave.
St. Catharines, Ontario
L2M 5V6

Published in the United States
Crabtree Publishing
PMB 59051
350 Fifth Avenue, 59th Floor
New York, New York 10118

CONTENTS

THE CITY CENTER

Welcome to Rome in 200 AD. It is the largest and most famous city in the world—one million people live here.

This is Rome from above. It is one of the most incredible cities in the world.

Finding your way

Rome has grown bigger and bigger over hundreds of years. Now it's a mess of thousands of streets, in which you can easily get lost. In the newer areas, however, streets have been built in a grid pattern that is easier to follow.

Colosseum

Forum

Circus Maximus

Slave city

You will see many slaves in Rome. Slaves cook, clean, and look after children. They even empty the jars that men and boys use as toilets in the streets!

The Forum of the Romans

The Forum is one of Rome's main meeting places. The crowded streets open out into a big space jammed with crowds of people shouting their business.

You can watch acrobats, listen to musicians play, and even have your fortune told.

We Romans have a vast empire stretching all over the world. People from all over the empire come to visit Rome.

5

WHERE TO STAY

The cheapest places to stay are apartment blocks called *insulae*. They can be dangerous. Criminals find *insulae* easy to rob. *Insulae* are crowded and can fall down without warning. Get a room on the ground floor or first floor, so you can get out if there is a fire.

Upscale

It is much nicer to stay in a house—there is less noise, for one thing. Richer people, such as **merchants**, live in houses with a courtyard in the middle and a backyard. We Romans call a house a *domus*.

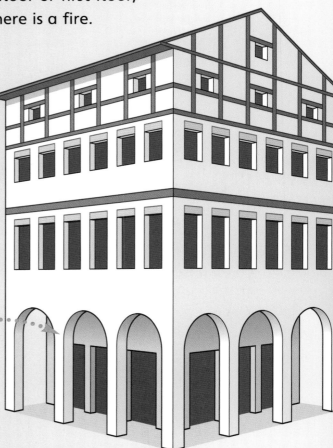

Insulae **are made of stone and wood. They often catch fire and burn down.**

Room for rent

People advertise rooms in their houses for travelers to rent. Look for a sign on the wall of the house.

The inside of a *domus* can be beautifully decorated with wall paintings and mosaics.

Five-star stays

Our richest citizens live like gods. They have town houses and also **villas** such as the one below. They are usually outside the city, away from all the noises and smells.

SHOPPING

Rome is a great place for shopping. We Romans built the Markets of **Trajan**—the world's first shopping mall. It has 150 offices and stores that sell things such as flowers, jewelry, wool, wine, and food.

Rainbow-colored mosaics

Some of these stores are beautiful. Pictures of the goods on sale are set into the walls or floors. They are made of tiny pieces of brightly colored tiles. These pictures are called mosaics.

Fish is very expensive in Rome. Wine is cheap.

Earning a living

Roman money is called *denarii*.
A Roman soldier earns about
450 *denarii* a year. It costs about
15 *denarii* to buy a pair of boots.

Shopping tips

- Look for stores in the bottom of buildings along the street.
- For the freshest food go to one of the markets held every nine days for all the farmers who live outside Rome.

Souvenirs

Some things you can buy on the streets:

- live animals in cages
- slaves
- silk from China
- wool from France
- spices from India

Romans use spices from India to add flavor to their food.

EATING OUT

We have thousands of fast-food stalls, called *thermopolia*. These stalls are open to the street. Their counters are filled with hot takeout food and drinks.

Olive oil is used to cook most foods in Rome.

Delicacies

Some of our favorite foods are:

- dolphin meatballs
- boiled parrot
- jellyfish omelets
- stuffed dormice
- crows

Bread snacks

You will see large bread ovens all over the city. We love bread and call it *panis* (right). We dip it in wine or olive oil and eat it as a snack because we do not eat a big meal until the late afternoon.

Banquets

If you are lucky you might be invited to a **banquet**. Banquets take place in people's houses. It is usual to eat at a banquet lying down on couches arranged around a table. Banquets can last for hours.

Slaves serve the food and wine at banquets.

Banquet manners

- Eat with your fingers.
- Take your own napkin.

11

CHARIOT RACES

Chariot racing is the most popular sport in Rome. Screaming crowds cheer on their heroes.

Chariot racing is a dangerous sport. Many horses and drivers die in crashes.

The Circus Maximus

The Circus Maximus is a huge stadium where people flock to see chariot racing. About 200,000 people can squeeze into the Circus Maximus.

A chariot driver races with the reins wrapped around his waist.

How do they do it?

Drivers stand on small wooden platforms fixed above the wheels of the chariots. They wrap the **reins** around their waists and then lean in different directions to control their horses.

Which team do you support?

- There are usually four chariot teams in a race.
- Each team has three chariots.
- The team colors are green, blue, white, or red.
- Fans wear team colors.
- The drivers usually race around the Circus Maximus seven times.

Top earners

Top chariot drivers can earn as much as a schoolteacher does in a year—for winning just one race!

13

GLADIATORS

About once a month you can see gladiators fight in the Colosseum. This is a massive oval arena called an **amphitheater**.

Up to 80,000 people can fit in the Colosseum.

How to take part

If you want to help decide if a gladiator lives or dies you'll need to learn a few words of **Latin**.

- *Mitte* means "Let him go."
- *Lugula!* means "Kill!"

Gladiators are trained to fight at special schools.

Gladiator guide

Gladiators are stars. They are also slaves and criminals. Here are four of the most popular types of gladiators.

- *Mirmillones* have a helmet with a fish crest, an oblong shield, and a sword. They can be put with a *Thracian* or a *Retiarius* to fight as a team.
- *Retiarii* have very few weapons—only a net and either a **trident** or a dagger.
- *Samnites* have a short sword, a helmet, and an oblong shield.
- *Thracians* have a curved sword and a round shield.

GUIDE TO GODS

The gods here in Rome all have superpowers. We pray to them and give **sacrifices** to make sure they stay here and protect us.

The walls of the Pantheon are 20 feet (6 m) thick so they can carry the huge weight of the dome.

The Pantheon

The **Pantheon** is the temple where all the main gods live. It is huge. The roof is a dome, like an open umbrella stuck on top of the building.

M·AGRIPPA·L·F·COSTERTIY

Pleasing the gods

Priests kill animals such as bulls or chickens. Then they cut them open. If the insides are healthy, the gods are happy. If the insides are unhealthy, the gods are angry.

Neptune is the Roman god of seas, horses, and earthquakes.

Top gods

Jupiter: king of the gods

Juno: queen of the gods

Venus: goddess of love

Diana: goddess of hunting/ the moon

Apollo: god of the sun

Mars: god of war

Minerva: goddess of wisdom

Neptune: god of the sea

Mercury: messenger of the gods

Animals such as bulls, like the one in this mosaic, are killed at specially built altars outside temples.

A LEISURELY BATH

Rome is a hot, smelly city, but there is an easy way to keep clean—take a bath! We have public baths that are the wonder of the world—up to 1,000 people can bathe at one time.

How to take a Roman bath

1. Take off your clothes and do a few exercises.
2. Then go into another room called the *tepidarium,* or "warm room," which is filled with hot air.
3. Next, go into the *calidarium,* or "hot room." It is so hot it is like being in a fire! Rub perfumed oil onto your skin and then scrape it off with a *strigil.*
4. Finally, jump into the *frigidarium*, which is a pool of freezing water.

A *strigil* is a scraper that clears away oil, sweat, dirt, and dead skin. It has a handle and a curved blade.

Some things to do at the baths

- Bathe!
- Do business
- Eat
- Read (baths have libraries)
- Have a beauty treatment
- Just relax!

There are almost 900 public baths in Rome!

IF YOU ARE ILL...

So many people live in Rome that illness can quickly spread through the city from person to person.

Stay well

If you feel unwell or are injured in a fall from a chariot, there is no hospital to go to. There is a hospital at the military camp, but only soldiers are allowed to use it.

Finding a doctor

Try to find a doctor who is a captured Greek slave—they are much better than Roman doctors. Some doctors even try to trick you. They ask for money for medicine that does not work.

Rich Romans often employ their own doctor. He is a servant who lives with them.

MEMPHI   GLEGORI

Avoid having an operation! Roman doctors have very basic surgical tools, such as the instruments shown above.

Pray

You can always go to a temple and pray to **Asklepios**, the god of medicine. Some doctors give you a prayer to go with your medicine to make it more powerful.

Bone drilling

Bone drills are used to get things such as weapons out of bones. They look like corkscrews. You do not get a painkiller when a doctor uses a bone drill on you.

GLOSSARY

amphitheater A large, circular building like a football stadium. Many forms of entertainment took place in amphitheaters

Asklepios The Greek god of medicine. The Romans decided to use him as their god of medicine, too

banquet A meal in which many courses of food are served over many hours

denarii Roman coins made of silver

Latin The language of Rome and the Roman Empire

merchants People who travel to buy and sell goods

mosaics Wall, floor, or ceiling pictures made up of tiny squares of colored tile, stone, or glass

Pantheon A temple built in Rome from about 125 AD, during the reign of the Emperor Hadrian

reins Thin lengths of leather fixed around a horse's head at one end and held at the other end by the person in control of the horse

sacrifices Killing animals in honor of the gods

Trajan Emperor from 98 to 117 AD. A great general and also known for his building projects in Rome

trident A spear with three spikes

villas The Roman name for rich people's houses in the country

FURTHER INFORMATION

Web sites

Find out all about Roman life and test your knowledge with some fun quizzes and word searches at:

www.historyonthenet.com/Romans/romansmain.htm

Find out more about what life was like in Roman times at:

www.pbs.org/empires/romans/empire/life.html

Books

Romans (Ancients in Their Own Words) by Michael Kerrigan. Benchmark Books (2010)

Ancient Communities: Roman LIfe. PowerKids Press (2010)

Life in Ancient Rome (People of the Ancient World) by Shilpa Mehta-Jones. Crabtree Publishing Company (2005)

Romans: Dress, Eat, Write and Play just like the Romans (Hands-on History) by Fiona Macdonald. Crabtree Publishing Company (2008)

INDEX